Against Morality

Rosanna McLaughlin

Contents

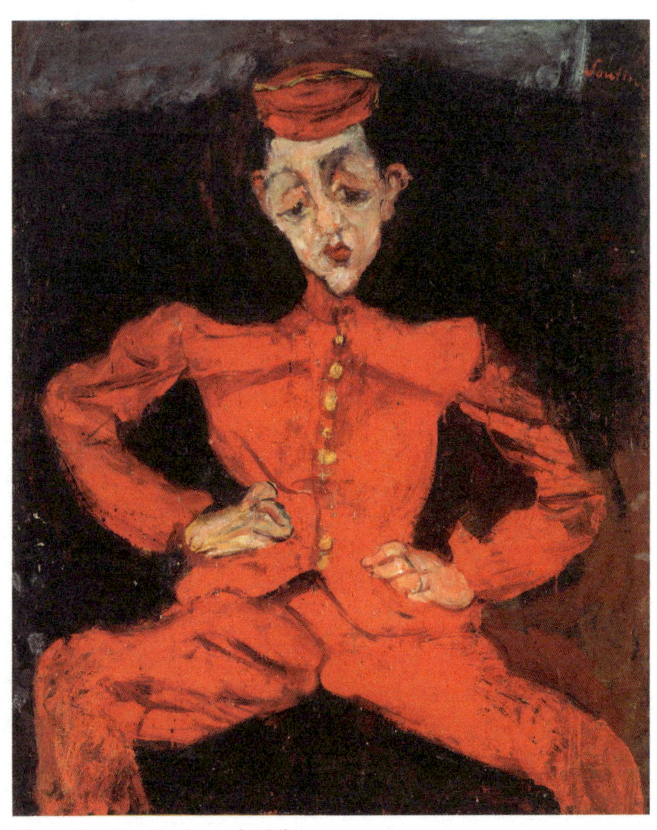

Chaïm Soutine, *Le Groom* (1925)

Off the Sofa

One rainy afternoon not so long ago, wrapped up in a blanket and enjoying the sweet sensation of avoiding a writing deadline, I found myself googling paintings by Chaïm Soutine. It's a pastime I have indulged regularly ever since visiting an exhibition of portraits Soutine made of hotel staff working on the French Riviera during the 1920s—paintings that combine such a mixture of tenderness and debasement that it is as if his brush is kissing and beating his subjects at the same time. I flicked through images of hopelessly innocent cooks and bellboys with complexions the color of raw sausage, ears that look as if they have been brutally yanked, bulging groins, fragile limbs, eyelids bruised and swollen with pink and gray paint. As I scrolled, I came across a review in *Frieze* magazine of the very show at Somerset House where I had first encountered Soutine's works in 2017. *Ah*, I thought, looking forward to immersing myself in the literature of his particular genius for kindly sadism.

Moments later it had all gone horribly wrong. My plan to float away on the wings of Soutine's twisted dream was disturbed by the words on the page. The artist, according to the review, had a "profoundly compassionate and humane eye," one that "sympathetically drifted to the underclass." As I read, I felt as if I had been sucked into the Upside Down, a surreal and unpleasant place where opposites are true. There was no mention of the violence or objectification coursing through Soutine's paint. Instead, the artist was described as bringing "dignity" to those at the bottom of the social order by celebrating "the richness of these otherwise forgotten lives." Finding myself utterly unable to marry the interpretation to the artworks, I began to worry that something had gone terribly wrong. *Am I having a stroke?* I wondered, clutching my blanket. I pinched my arms and legs: no numbness. I focused my eyes on the branch of a tree: vision intact. I even read a few lines out loud to confirm that my speech was operating as it ought to. Relieved to find my cognitive function unimpaired, I was left to contend with a deeply unsettling question: Why would anyone reframe Soutine as a saintly advocate for social and representational justice?

After all, this was the very same Soutine whose skill as a painter-cum-butcher inspired Francis Bacon's nightmarish visions. It is certainly of no benefit to *his* legacy to have his most interesting qualities sloughed off and dumped beyond the margins, his kinks sanded down into a smooth and anodyne veneer. It is also of dubious benefit to the working class, the demographic the review claims Soutine is championing, who are asked to swallow the reframing of objectification as charity and embrace a voyeur as a savior. What makes Soutine's portraits so good, so special, so *moving*, is that they mix brutality with affection. It is because of their unsettling qualities, their fundamental amorality, that they are able to speak to the complexity of human relationships, the erotics of power differentials, the violence tangled up in longing, the extent to which care and cruelty are bedfellows. Few of us are outright psychopaths, after all, but all of us must reckon with the fine and often fictional line between desire and exploitation.

Since giving up alcohol, my strategy for coping with moments of unexpected distress is to dunk myself in viciously hot water. Feeling unsettled, and not wishing to forfeit my sobriety, I dragged myself off the sofa and ran a bath. I lowered myself in, and as my body turned bright pink, as my fingers puckered and I felt the slow hammer of my pulse thumping in my neck, as the stress departed from my body like an exorcised spirit, rising upward with the spangled curls of steam, my thoughts on the matter began to crystallize…

The review itself, I realized, was entirely unremarkable. It was the kind of piece put out daily and by the dozen by art publications around the world, churned out for barely any money; writing designed to place the author, reader, and publication on what is frequently referred to as "the right side of history"; writing that has neither the time nor the financial incentive to get under the skin of an artwork; writing that is fundamentally self-conscious and risk-averse, so caught up in saying the right thing that it fails to account for what is staring it in the face; writing that any critic would produce if they allowed themselves to be swept along by the powerful tide of the art-world status quo. It was precisely the review's ordinariness that struck me as worthy of exploration, for it was typical of an insistence that artists (alive or dead) conform to a moral code. This cultural ideology has had the arts in a chokehold for the best part of a decade and has profound implications for how we engage with art, what we expect from it, how we conceive of its purpose, and what role we permit it to fulfill.

Feeling the whoosh of inspiration, I hauled my body from the water, dried my hands on the crumpled T-shirt I had left on the floor, and began making the notes that would eventually become this essay—an essay that is, in essence, a call for an art, and an appreciation of art, that transcends simple moralizing in order to speak to the complex and messy reality of what it is to be alive.

I
The Importance of Amorality

Art excels when it shows us things that aren't easily put into words. Those concepts, emotions, and psychological states that we have neither the time nor capacity to contemplate in our day-to-day lives, and which other means of communication may fail to convey. Better yet is the kind of art that can complicate ideas that otherwise appear to us as black and white, art that cuts through our assumptions and reveals their limitations, getting us to feel and see the world again, to see further. Most art, of course, will never come anywhere near achieving this, for the obvious reason that most of it isn't particularly good. This isn't to suggest that making and discussing it is a pointless pursuit. Far from it. The tiny percentage of art that is capable of moving us, of extending our field of perception, makes the limited nature of the majority of cultural production worthwhile. Hints of depth can be found in the most tedious of work, and the intention to reach for something more, even if that reaching is destined for failure, is a reminder that a destination exists beyond our current capacities of comprehension. Art history may be full of talk about perspective and horizon, yet the greatest space that art opens up is not within the pictorial field but inside the viewer.

When I talk about the tiny percentage of art that is capable of transporting us, of making us feel and think in different ways, I am talking about the kind of art that gives form to the complex experience of being human, of walking the earth in a decaying suit of flesh, attempting to figure out what the point of existence is, why we think and want as we do, what the symbols and objects that surround us mean, how to balance our own desires and needs with the desires and needs of others, how to reconcile ourselves to those who have come before us and those who will come after us, how to cope with the humiliations and ecstasies of having a body, with the beauty and horror of looking, with the anxiety and confusion of being in the world, with the vast potential of all the things we do not and may never know, all the while wading through the mundane swamp of life with the unbearable burden of our ever-approaching demise strapped to our backs like a rucksack full of bricks.

By necessity, such a transportive and revelatory art does not settle for confirming what we think we already know, for telling rather than showing. It does not simply reflect a predetermined set of ideas or opinions back to us or smack us around the head with a rule book. It is not content to operate as an illustration or signpost to "good" politics or approved outlooks and modes of expression. Instead, it provokes complicated, contradictory, and ambivalent feelings and ideas that are often impossible to resolve, and which—precisely because of the lack of resolution they offer—remain in our thoughts, acting against the tyranny of easy consolations and pushing us onward. This is the reason why I continue to seek out Soutine's paintings almost a decade after first encountering them. His tender and tenderized cooks and bellboys require that I give over to the world of the work, that I make room for contradictory and conflicting values and emotions.

For similar reasons, I have always preferred Hieronymus Bosch's depictions of hell to his depictions of heaven. Demons spit-roasting humans, beetles riding men, a malevolent cock and balls made from the ears of a giant and the blade of a knife; the damned beaten with hammers, boiled in vats, and drowned in alcohol. Bosch's cornucopia of perversions may have been justified in the name of piety, as a warning to unrepentant sinners of the fate that awaits them. But its centuries-old charisma

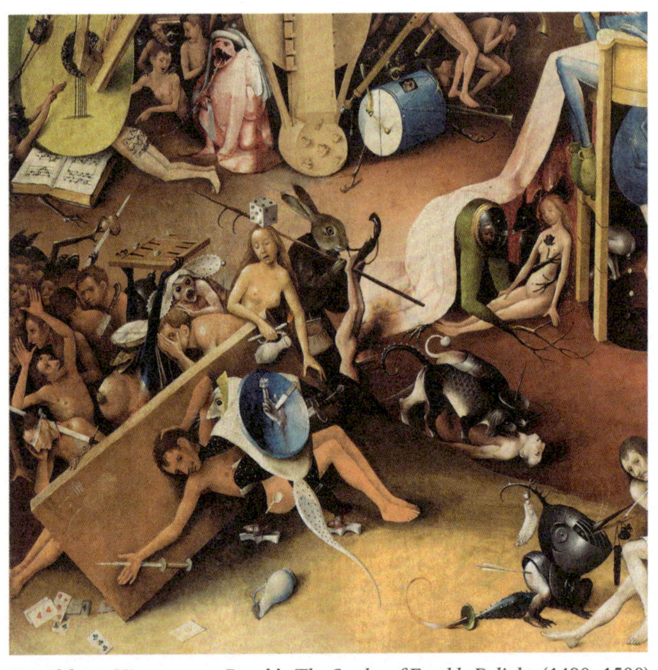

Detail from Hieronymus Bosch's *The Garden of Earthly Delights* (1490–1500)

is the product of the fundamental tension between religious fervor and Bosch's obsessive indulgence in depravity, a tension that vibrates like particles in boiling water, creating a transfer of energy from artwork to viewer. How much less dynamic are scenes of heaven! As a place where nothing lurks half-seen in the shadows, nobody is doing unspeakable things, love is untainted by cruelty, innocence is uncorrupted, and power is only wielded as a force for universal good, heaven may provide a standard to aspire to, but it is by necessity free from the lusty, contradictory, and morally ambivalent experience of being human.

I do not advocate for such artworks because I myself long to be spit-roasted by devils or tenderized by a kindly sadist, as promising as those scenarios may sound. I advocate for them because exposure to conflicting drives and desires asks us to consider our own complicated feelings, our own attitudes to risk, power, love, and desire, our own stakes in the unending war between id and superego, between the "I want" and the "I must not." It requires a capacity for self-reflection, for openness, without which art loses the possibility of enabling transformation and transcendence, and of connecting with the human spirit (however sick that spirit may be)—concepts that seem to have fallen out of favor in recent times, but without which art is reduced to little more than esoteric cultural or political commentary and social posturing. If we create a culture in which we are no longer able or willing to give ourselves over to artworks and instead approach them as illustrations of predefined and preapproved messages, they are stripped of their vitality along with their power. In the words of Oscar Wilde: "If a man approaches a work of art with any desire to exercise authority over it and the artist, he approaches it in such a spirit that he cannot receive any artistic impression from it at all."

Despite what we stand to lose by rejecting the complexities of art, over the past decade or so there has been a concerted attempt to make art communicate clear and approvable messages, to clean up the canon, to preach a sanctioned set of tenets, ironing out any of the ambivalences that make art *move*. Morality has become the central pillar, the justification for art, the bar by which we measure whether something is good or bad. So much so, that the worth of an artwork is now apparently synonymous with the worthiness of its maker.

One of the most striking facets of this attachment to goodness is the desire for art to transform itself into something more obviously socially useful, in order to prove its value: to become activism, community-oriented architecture, archive, outreach, social work, legal advocacy. Sometimes, the space that the fine arts are able to provide for such projects results in creative responses to real-world issues. Forensic Architecture's reconstructions of war crimes and investigations into the abuses of governments, for example, have been used to prosecute human rights violations. But for every project that contributes something of note, there are countless instances of art as activism or advocacy that fetishize social justice, and whose usefulness to the people they purportedly serve is far less clear than the desire to uphold a fantasy of the artist as guardian angel of community cohesion.

In the United Kingdom, there is widespread dependence on public funding bodies to finance cultural projects that are unlikely to attract the support of the commercial art world. Such organizations tend to reward art that claims to contribute to the social good—being unwilling, and perhaps unable, to judge a proposal based on aesthetics alone. Anyone who has worked in the arts is likely to be familiar with the stories. During my wife's first week in the dissection room as a medical student, an artist was present during her anatomy classes, undertaking exactly the kind of interdisciplinary project supposedly enacted in a spirit of community that is catnip for funding bodies. Sitting in the room while the trainee medics fainted and vomited, stared death in the face, and attempted to come to terms with mortality and the high stakes of the job for which they were training, she asked them to bring in socks with holes in them so that she could darn them while they worked—supposedly a gesture of care, repair, and solidarity. (Perhaps unsurprisingly, given the more pressing matters at hand, nobody gave her anything.) A whole generation of art school graduates—whose ranks have swollen to vast proportions as universities continue to increase admission numbers—attempting to make a career are shaping their work to fulfill the criteria of grant applications. Roland Barthes's idea that the author is dead and buried has taken a turn for the administrative: we now live in a world where artworks are rubber-stamped by people sitting in Teams meetings, cross-checking applications against a ten-point plan for morally upstanding art.

This fetish for the aesthetics of social utility and advocacy has created a politically homogenous cultural field, marked by a deep-seated mistrust of ambivalence. For the past decade or so, we have lived in a cultural environment with an extraordinary intolerance of anyone or anything that doesn't arrive with its good politics, its solidarity with the oppressed, tattooed across its forehead—and sees no qualms with tattooing such a politics onto the corpses of cultural history if it better suits the demands of the present.

Intolerance to ambiguity is certainly not a phenomenon limited to the fine arts. I witnessed it unfold in real time when I went to watch the film *Tár* at the cinema with a friend in 2023. Directed by Todd Haynes, *Tár* tells the story of a powerful, corrupt, and mesmerically

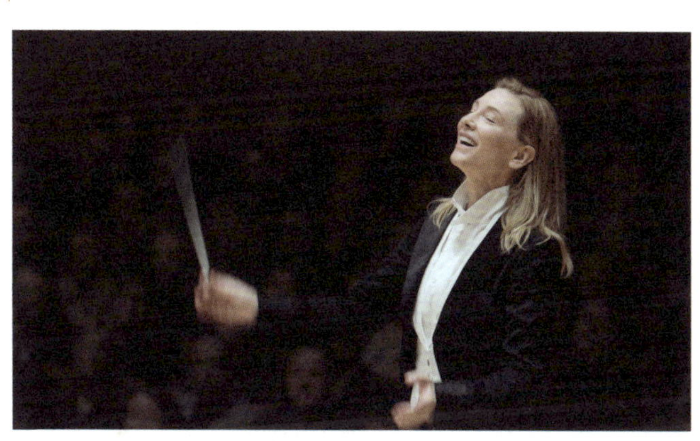

Still from *Tár* (2022)

attractive lesbian conductor played by Cate Blanchett. Partway through the film, my friend and I were disturbed from our appreciation of Blanchett by the noise of multiple viewers tutting and sighing as they walked out, apparently offended by a scene in which her character, Lydia Tár, lays into a student during a lecture, in response to their dismissal of the composer Bach for his ostensible moral failings. "As a BIPOC, pangender person, I would say Bach's misogynistic life makes it kind of impossible for me to take his music seriously," the student says. In response, Tár launches into a grandiose speech about the foolishness of rejecting greatness on the grounds of identity and tells them that "the narcissism of small differences leads to the most boring conformity," a verbal tirade that continues until the student gets up and leaves, calling her a "fucking bitch" on the way out. The scene is effective precisely because it holds two opposing views at the same time. The student is censorious, hypersensitive, and self-involved, determined to play judge and jury with the canon. Their teacher is a callous and overbearing egotist who is fundamentally lacking in empathy, and who, the film goes on to show, is willing to jeopardize the lives and careers of the younger women she seduces to protect her own. Part of what saves the film from being a paint-by-numbers story of snowflakes versus the corrupt establishment is Blanchett's exuberant charisma, which means that the character she plays cannot be dismissed as a pig of a man, a caricature of disgusting, villainous masculinity in the mold of Harvey Weinstein or any of the other MeToo monsters. Haynes pushes the viewer to experience their own desire for Tár, to experience the uncomfortable position of both rooting for, and being drawn to, a deeply dubious figure. What better way to express the visceral appeal of power and sexual charm, in order to exemplify how and why such figures are often able to abuse their authority, than to cast an actor as revered and enchanting as Cate Blanchett in the role? The exodus from the cinema, I was left to presume, was caused by an unwillingness among certain viewers to countenance themselves, their intentions, or their desires as anything other than one-dimensionally pure.

Narrow-mindedness toward the film extended beyond the screening. After its release, *The Times* ran an interview with a real-life conductor named Marin Alsop, in which she claimed, "I was offended as a woman, I was offended as a conductor, I was offended as a lesbian," describing the decision to portray an abusive female conductor as "heartbreaking." "There are so many actual, documented men this film could have been based on but, instead, it puts a woman in the role but gives her all the attributes of those men. That feels antiwoman." To take such a position is to engage in a tremendous feat of cultural flattening. It is to suggest that there is no difference between fiction and reality, that art should serve no other purpose than to promote a set of prescribed social and political messages, and that marginalized groups should be represented along highly limited terms. It is to imagine that no member of a group deemed oppressed could abuse their power and suggests a world in which every lesbian shares the same personality traits and moral values—a gross simplification. Because there are, of course, a great many "bad" lesbians out there, just as there are a sizeable number of Black and Latin American voters in the United States who support Trump, and racists from the Global South, all of whom upset liberal expectations regarding the correlation between identity and behavior. *Tár* shows us a lesbian who has succeeded against the odds in a male-dominated field, a magnetically attractive force of nature who basks in her own brilliance; it also shows us a person high on power and willing to sacrifice others at the altars of status and ego. That the film requires the viewer to hold both aspects of her character simultaneously, to desire her and abhor her, is surely a complexity worthy of celebration rather than reproach.

II
Liberal Realism

The current obsession with flattening culture, the attachment to simplistic moralizing, the deadening of art, are all features of what I call "Liberal Realism." Like Socialist Realism before it, Liberal Realism is the product of a culture that demands its ideology be unambiguously reflected in its art. The Soviets mandated that art must celebrate the ideals of a socialist society, an idea introduced at the First Congress of Soviet Writers in 1934. (By the time the Second Congress came around, most of the writers had been murdered during the Great Purge.) Soviet Realism was an art of comrades in arms enraptured by the spirit of revolution; strong, happy workers forging scythes and planning for the collective future; idyllic scenes of communal childrearing facilities or children handing bouquets of flowers to Daddy

Stalin in bucolic landscapes. Death could only be depicted if valiant, and images of abject poverty and state suppression—or anything that risked undermining the prescribed vision, any ambivalent portrayal of life—were outlawed on pain of death.

While Liberal Realism is just as allergic to anything that strays from the script, it is the product of a very different age: a time when, across the political spectrum, identity is capital and culture is shaped by competing claims of victimhood; a time when the state is downstream from the market and social media, imagination has been drowned by the sheer scale of available information, and visions of the future largely involve fantastical stories we tell ourselves about the past. In this regard, Liberal Realism is also the progeny of what Mark Fisher called Capitalist Realism: a form of societal conditioning that precludes the possibility that any future exists outside of capitalism, creating a political and cultural sphere marked by an utter lack of imagination. Today, in place of the gulag there is only cancellation, and its attendant PR opportunities for the obnoxious and narcissistic can relaunch themselves as indomitable torchbearers for free speech—a transformation exemplified by Russell Brand, who, having been canceled by the liberal left following multiple accusations of sexual assault, walked into the open arms of the libertarian right. The legacy of deconstruction, and our triumphant

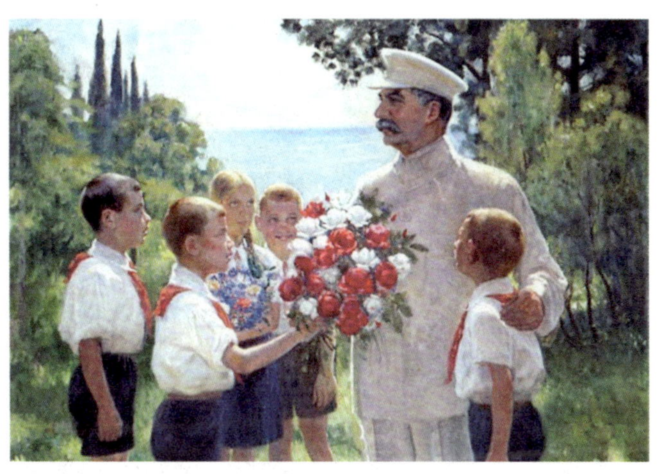

Boris Vladimirski, *Roses for Stalin* (1949)

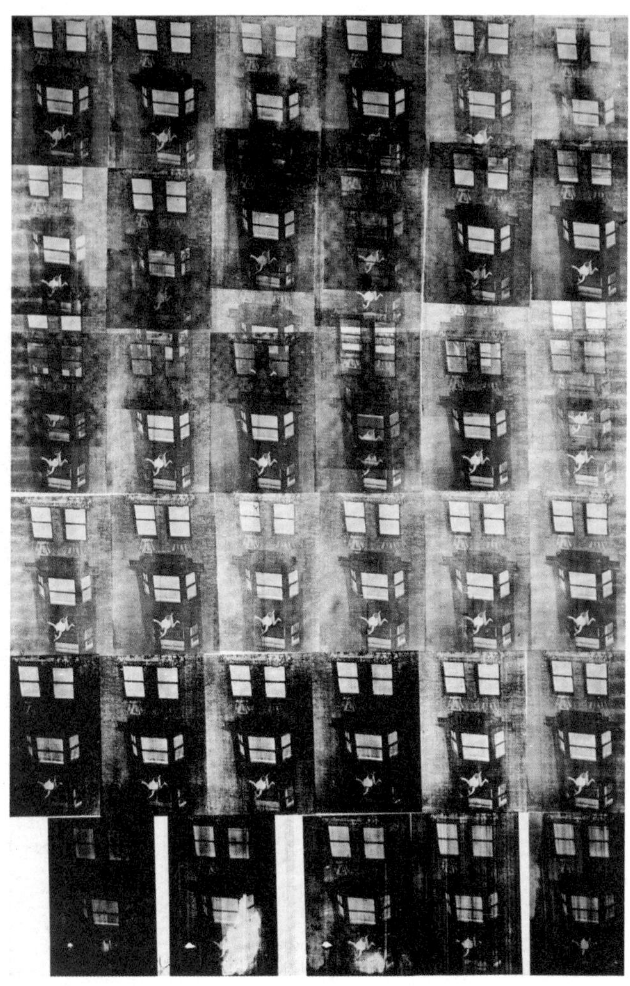

Andy Warhol, *A Woman's Suicide* (1962)

ability to pick at the seams of ideas and histories, to point out what's wrong with the world we have inherited—and, indeed, to point out the flaws of our peers—without the possibility of rehabilitation has created a culture adept at taking things apart, but impotent when it comes to putting things together. Liberal Realism is the art of those who sit in the educated rubble of civilization, among the structures and narratives we have so expertly disassembled, unable and afraid to countenance building something new, of risking putting something out in the world—unless its meaning and politics have already been assessed, confirmed, and approved—because we know all too well how easy it is to tear a thing to shreds.

It follows, then, that Liberal Realist art is timid, defensive, and rule-bound. Confident only when pointing out errors and injustices, when anointing heroes and villains, it has no appetite for genuine transgression or experimentation, no appetite for risking anything as exposing as expression. Its art is expected to reflect a certain set of values, one that the viewer already has, or that the artist and curatorial team expects them to acquire as they engage with an exhibition: anti-patriarchal, anti-racist, anti-individual, committed to collective action and intersectional politics, inclusive, educational, and dedicated to rectifying inequalities past and present by making space for the voices of the marginalized. You may well think that these seem like worthwhile values to adhere to in life. Indeed, in our dealings with friends, family, colleagues, and neighbors, and when applied to political governance, they can be values worth fighting for. (They are also values that are often conspicuously absent from the policies and actions of so-called center-left Western political parties, despite lip service to the contrary, a reality that is surely playing its part in their loosening grip on power.) The problem is that they make for a deeply prescriptive and limited model of art—one with a tendency to reduce art to an illustration of a pre-defined political message, and to reduce the artist to a predefined set of biographical markers.

Unwilling to leave anything open to interpretation, Liberal Realist art is profoundly reliant on curatorial devices that explain to viewers why an artist's work is important—framing that often relies heavily on simplistic accounts of artists' identities. Biography is a story we can be told, one that can be controlled and editorialized (particularly if an artist is dead), and from which we can glean whether or not it is appropriate to be interested in (or to identify with) the work on display. To simply look at an artwork, to be left to interpret messages and gestures with no clear instructions, is not only unattractive in an era when clarity is a prerequisite: to many it has become unthinkable. Thus, the viewer is told what to think and why, artworks become illustrations for the meta-narrative of biography, and artists and their subjects ciphers for social-justice narratives, their work simplified to better meet the needs of the present.

In the name of the good, all manner of liberties may be taken. During the days before the first COVID-19 lockdown came into force, I visited the Andy Warhol retrospective at Tate Modern in London. The galleries were packed with sweaty, frantic bodies, and it felt as though half the city had congregated to see Warhol's *Marilyn* and electric chairs one last time before the human species was wiped out. In the first room, I stopped to read the wall text. It described how Warhol "provided a safe space for queer culture"—an extraordinary act of cultural revisionism, and one that set the tone for an exhibition that claimed Warhol as an artist fighting the good fight on behalf of vulnerable people and minority groups. This was an about-turn from the narrative of Warhol the art-bro that had been pedaled previously, but it was no less rickety. What "safe space" did Warhol provide for the drug-addled muses who featured in his films? Or for Olga Cassonava, the fourteen-year-old girl photographed falling to her death from an apartment block, an image from which he made the screenprint *A Woman's Suicide* (1962)? This was the same Andy Warhol whose interest in sex, death, and exploitation made him a formidable force; a man who filmed a slew of young and vulnerable fame-seekers, often high on drugs and desperate for the limelight. It is precisely Warhol's voyeurism, his insatiable lust for images of sex, death, and the cold, dazzling heart of Western consumerism, his vampiric ability to suck the life from those around him and transform it into art, his ruthlessness as a talent scout, that make him, and his work, so astonishing. His art is deeply amoral, and not at all interested in providing succor for the vulnerable. Recasting him as an angel is only of use to those who wish to frame cultural institutions as beacons of tolerance and diversity in the present day.

Artemisia Gentileschi is another artist who has been subjected to a dubious moralistic glow-up. Despite being wildly successful during her lifetime and working as a court painter at the highest level, she has latterly been transformed into a cipher for MeToo feminism and the paradigmatic example of the "overlooked woman artist." Her most famous painting, *Judith Slaying Holofernes* (ca. 1620), is now widely interpreted as an autobiographical response to her own rape by the painter Agostino Tassi—a deeply unpleasant man who was convicted at trial of the crime, having previously served time for arranging the murder of his wife—the woman shown chopping off a man's head assumed to be Artemisia herself.

Over the past decade, media platforms and art institutions alike have squeezed the air out of Artemisia's legacy. "The Woman Who Took Revenge in Oil," ran a headline in *The Guardian*. "In the wake of the [Brett] Kavanaugh hearings, I've developed a new self-care routine: I put on a sheet mask, cue up some soothing music, and look at paintings of murderous women," began an article on the website Artsy, which goes on to describe Artemisia's *Judith Slaying Holofernes* as a "portrayal of the justice that she herself was denied."

The thing is, we will never know just how biographical Artemisia intended the painting to be. The figure of Judith looks very much like Artemisia herself, but Artemisia tended to include herself in her paintings rather than hiring models. What we do know is that the painting is based on a Biblical story in which Judith, a Jewish widow, seduces and kills Holofernes, an Assyrian general, during the siege of the city of Bethulia, helping the Israelites win in the war against their enemies. We also know that the slaying of Holofernes was a standard subject among Renaissance and Baroque painters, depicted by Botticelli, Mantegna, Michelangelo, Cranach the Elder, Caravaggio, and many others, before Artemisia took it on. Indeed, Artemisia's Judith has a similar expression on her face to Caravaggio's, which likely inspired it: focused, businesslike, and oddly unmoved given the nature of the act. She could just as well be butchering a goat at the end of a hard day's work as ending the life of a mortal enemy. Yet when an exhibition of Artemisia's work was staged at the National Gallery in London in 2020, the viewer was instructed to view the painting as a direct representation of the artist's personal experiences.

A document from Agostini Tassi's trial for rape was even on display near the beginning of the exhibition, making clear how her art should be interpreted: as indivisible from the traumas of her private life. The obsession with moral and biographical narratives is so totalizing, so compelling, and so flattening, that it compromises our ability to focus on Artemisia's art, obscuring the visual language she created by transforming her work into an illustration of a politics created in the present. In the name of "saving" her legacy, the very thing to which she dedicated her life is at risk of being compromised.

III
Heroes and Villains

Every era finds in the past those things that it craves, and the meaning of art necessarily changes through time. To stop this from happening is neither possible nor desirable. The past is a material we shape, a myth we tell ourselves to underpin our conception of the present, a legacy we edit to create the ancestry we would prefer to have. This is as true for the analysand on the therapist's couch as it is for the constant work of canon-building within the arts. Aby Warburg noted this very phenomenon in connection to the excavation of a Roman copy of a Greek statue known as the Laocoön: a highly melodramatic and erotic scene in which the muscular, writhing figures of a priest and his two sons are attacked by giant sea snakes. When the Laocoön was discovered in Rome in 1506, the era's anti-quity-obsessed artists found in its bombastic and emotive flair exactly the kind of historical precedent they craved in order to justify banishing the staid aesthetic of the Middle Ages and ushering in the flamboyant aesthetic of the Baroque. As Warburg wrote, "It was a revelation of something that Italians had long sought—and therefore found—in the art of the ancient world: extremes of gestural and physiognomical expression, stylized in tragic sublimity." Yet the same artists could just have easily found countless examples of ancient art that contained no such theatrical abandon, that embodied values entirely opposed to those of the Baroque, and which could have been used to justify a completely different cultural pathway.

When it comes to the past, as Warburg suggests, we find what we are looking for. And so it is that in recent years it has become par for the course to describe artists such as Soutine and Warhol as empathetic social workers, and to embrace the sight of Judith slicing into Holofernes's throat as a representation of women overcoming the patriarchy, of Artemisia Gentileschi herself taking down her abuser, an overlooked woman taking down the entire art-historical canon to boot, taking down bad men everywhere—and not as a virtuoso display of skill by a celebrated artist responding to a standard theme. Much like how science fiction's speculative visions of the future throw into relief the anxieties and aspirations of the present, recognizing the extent to which we retroactively project ideas onto the past enables us to

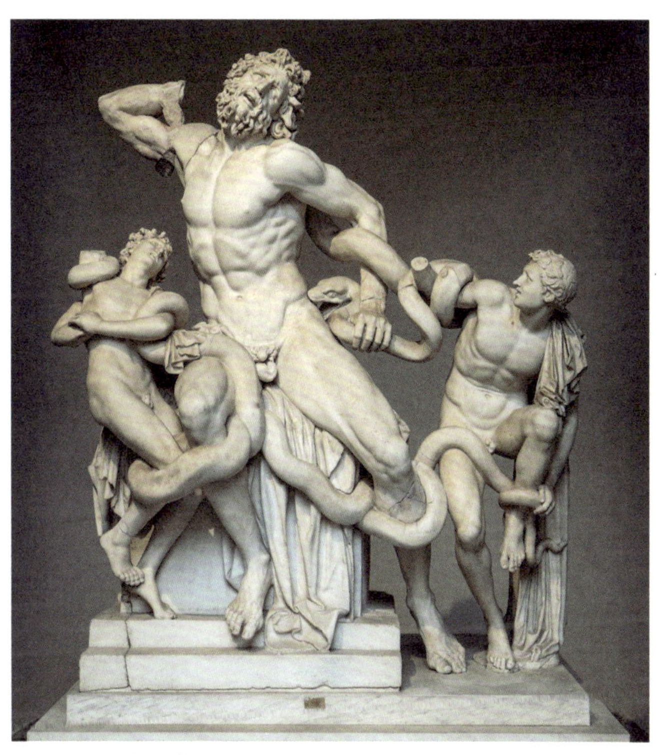

Agesander, Athenodoros, and Polydorus, *Laocoön and His Sons*
(ca. 27 BC–68 AD)

better understand the motivations and attitudes of the present. Liberal Realism's penchant for revisionism, and for moralizing, reveals a talent for cognitive dissonance and a deep anxiety about leaving anything open to interpretation.

Sometimes, the fear of ambivalence leads to public displays of paranoia, a notable example of which was the debacle surrounding the international touring exhibition of Philip Guston's work. In 2020, anxiety over the responses to Guston's depictions of cartoonlike figures akin to Ku Klux Klansmen resulted in the delay of the show "until a time at which we think that the powerful message of social and racial justice that is at the center of Philip Guston's work can be more clearly interpreted," to quote a statement signed by the directors of all four institutions set to host the exhibition—the National Gallery of Art in Washington, DC, the Museum of Fine Arts in Houston, Tate Modern in London, and the Museum of Fine Arts in Boston. When the exhibition eventually began touring (by 2022, the audience was presumed to be ready for that "powerful message"), certain curatorial decisions had been made to frame the show and control the work's reception. For the Boston leg, as Paul Keegan wrote in the *London Review of Books*, the show opened "with leaflets on emotional preparedness ('name your feelings') written by an onsite trauma specialist, plus an emergency exit ramp ahead of the most offending room, and video montages of life-and-times historical footage, replete with horrors, to which Guston's imagery must appear accountable."

When the show traveled to Tate Modern in London in 2023, there was no trauma specialist on hand to offer therapy to viewers, but pains were taken to convince the audience of Guston's good politics, framing his work as anti-racist. The truth, as Keegan suggests, is far more complex. The paintings do not offer anything like a clear political position. The inanity of Guston's hooded figures—painted in pig-pink and in Guston's childish style, sitting around blasting cigarettes, making art, and driving cars—is both troubling and ridiculous, suggesting the extent to which racism is unexceptional in America, and to which the figure of the Klansman was embedded in Guston's own imagination, knocking around with the other ephemera of modern American life. The paintings do not tell you what to think about the KKK, nor do they reaffirm any feelings the viewer may already have toward them. Instead, they show you a troubled psychological state, one that cannot be reduced to politically agreeable soundbites.

One of the calling cards of Liberal Realism is the propensity to dress up self-serving tendencies as moral superiority. The reframing of Guston as anti-racist primarily served the institutions that had agreed to show his work (not to mention those that have his works in their

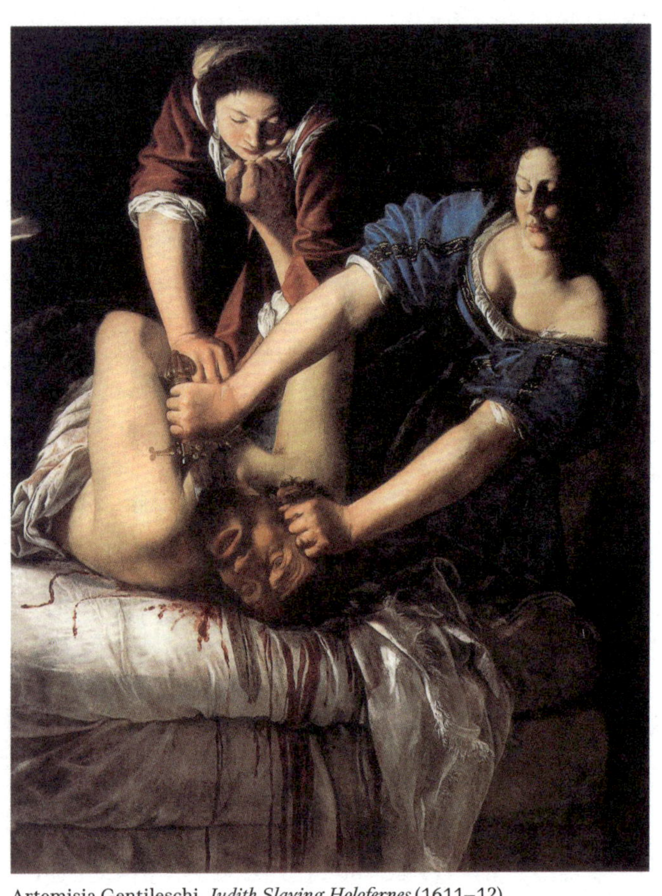

Artemisia Gentileschi, *Judith Slaying Holofernes* (1611–12)

collections). It served the market, too, as one of the major sellers of the twentieth century could be cleaned up and made presentable according to the rules of contemporary discourse. It did not serve the viewers, who were patronized by the dubious revisionism, and who were faced with the prospect of viewing Guston's work in environments hostile to taking the artworks on their own terms. It certainly did not serve Guston's legacy. Worst of all, in its triumphalist attitude of having "solved" the problem of racism in his paintings, it relieved audiences from having to contend with the uncomfortable notion that racism is a part of everyday life, as quotidian as cigarettes and cars, and part of their own psychological makeup.

Often, the very people Liberal Realism claims to champion are forced into inflexible stereotypes and caged by simplistic narratives. This is apparent in the much-abused category of "overlooked women artists," who must continue to be labeled as overlooked even when books have been written about them and exhibitions of their work staged. The artist Dora Maar is one such casualty of the regime. "Rare photographs by Dora Maar cast Picasso's tormented muse in a new light," ran the headline of an article in *The Observer* in 2024, an article that frames Maar as a damsel in distress, an artist cruelly overshadowed by Picasso—even though she herself was the subject of a major retrospective of her work at Tate Modern in 2020. The very people who claim to be releasing Maar from Picasso's captivity, rescuing her from obscurity and torment, are the ones who insist on mentioning her only in relation to him, and who are bent on trapping her in the narrative of the overlooked woman.

The prize for the most dubious causism surely goes to the treatment of Ana Mendieta—an artist who has posthumously been transformed into an art-world martyr, the nuance stripped out of her oeuvre and replaced with popular stories surrounding her death. Mendieta fell from an apartment block in New York in 1985, and many people believe that her husband, the artist Carl Andre, pushed her—he was found not guilty of second-degree murder in 1988. Today, the blood she utilized in her performances is regularly conflated with the blood shed when she died. (Those protesting the display of Andre's work at Tate Modern in 2016, on the grounds that the museum was lionizing a murderer, arrived with their arms dipped in red paint, a reference both to her artwork and to her death; "Ana Mendieta: Death of an Artist Foretold in Blood," ran the headline of an article in *The Observer*.) It has been transmogrified into a symbol of white patriarchal violence enacted on the body of a brown woman, and as a connection, along with her frequent use of feathers and other natural materials, to her lost homeland through the spiritual practice of Santería.

Mendieta, however, was a far more complex character than the mythology gives her credit for. She was a child refugee who fled Cuba for the United States, who rose to prominence against the odds with an extraordinary force of will, and who died at a tragically young age under dubious circumstances. She also began life as a member of a powerful Cuban family and is a relative of a former president. Her artwork can certainly be understood as a quest for belonging by a woman displaced from one culture to another. But her invocation of Santería was not a return to her own native customs. Santería is practiced by the Black ancestors of African slaves, and, in the Caribbean, Mendieta's family—as a scholar at the University of the West Indies once put it to me in no uncertain terms—would most certainly be seen as white. Such cultural nuances do not enter the discussion of Mendieta's art or life because they upset the narrative. How could a woman of color be involved in cultural appropriation—and when is cultural appropriation deemed worthy of celebration? What are the signs and symbols that appeal to the displaced, to those searching for authenticity and connection? How could her work be read as anything other than confessional ethnography? How could a woman who is white in one context be brown in another?

Rather than dealing with the complexities of Mendieta's work—complexities that contribute to its overwhelming charismatic force—the attention is placed, almost exclusively, on her death. All manner of art-world grifters have piggybacked on the morbid mythology.

Over and again, the "secret" of Ana Mendieta's death is revealed, giving any unscrupulous journalist, artist, or curator the chance to role-play as her savior. There is, perhaps, no better example of this than the 2022 Sony-backed podcast *Death of an Artist*, in which curator Helen Molesworth wheels the tale of Mendieta and Andre's doomed marriage out for another spin, giving it the true-crime treatment.

Over the course of six episodes, Molesworth frames herself as a woman on a mission to break the oppressive silence around Andre's suspected role in Mendieta's death—no matter the professional cost. While dredging through what are in fact the now-familiar details of the trial and its aftermath, she describes her own political awakening. In the wake of MeToo and Black Lives Matter, the former Andre fangirl, who recalls percolating with joy at the sight of his bricks and floor tiles in her youth, learns to curb her enthusiasm for a man accused of murdering his wife, a Cuban refugee, by throwing her out the window.

Death of an Artist makes for a predictable, if unintentional, portrait of an art establishment in the midst of a protracted identity crisis—rejecting the canon it worked to secure, and publicly pledging allegiance to a new doctrine in which, as Molesworth says, "identity matters." Yet while the podcast is framed as a quest for justice in Mendieta's name, in reality it is a lazy rehashing of a grim episode underpinned by a debatable relationship to the ethics it supposedly upholds. The silence that Molesworth says inspired her to action is by now a fallacy. You would be hard-pressed to find an art student today who doesn't think of Mendieta and her death when Andre's name is mentioned, or vice versa. Over the past forty years, countless articles have been written, books published, academic theses submitted, protests at the display of Andre's work staged. A popular, macabre folklore has emerged—one that Molesworth mines, indulging novelistic embellishments and hearsay. The podcast includes an often-repeated anecdote about the pictures at an exhibition falling off the walls when Andre and Mendieta first met, as if this were a sign of trouble to come—rather than an inadvisable choice of adhesive. A recording of Andre saying he is no longer able to lift heavy loads while making his work—an innocuous and rather dull reflection on aging—is used to invoke the image of him throwing Mendieta to her death. A woman who suffered a serious brain injury, and subsequently believed herself to be psychic, relays a premonition she had that Andre would kill Mendieta.

By now, surely, another kind of conversation needs to be had. Mendieta's death raises many unanswered questions that are worthy of more than self-serving and corny attention. What do we do when it is believed that a miscarriage of justice has taken place, one that belongs to a wider pattern of societal oppression? When should the cultural sector step in, and, if it does, who is assuming the authority to pass judgment? The same questions hang over the MeToo movement, which has largely stalled at the point of recounting instances of abuse, first as testimony, then as a vampiric cultural product that feeds on the spectacle of the cruelty it claims to uncover. (Marilyn Monroe's treatment in the 2022 film *Blonde*, and Monica Lewinsky's in the 2021 series *Impeachment: American Crime Story*, are but two examples. It would be no surprise to discover an Ana Mendieta biopic is in the works; by now the story writes itself.)

The dilemma of where we go from here will not be solved by repeating hearsay and role-playing detective. It requires a good-faith engagement with complex societal questions, a desire to move beyond treating the past as a theater of trauma to repeat ad nauseam. But this, of course, is not how Liberal Realism works.

Cripplingly self-conscious and imaginatively stunted, Liberal Realist culture traps artists and viewers in simplistic stories of heroes and villains and has no investment in what liberation from this binary might look like. Even as "trailblazers" and "rebels" of the modern era are lauded and the "enemies" of good causes pilloried—often in moronic ways, as exemplified by the exhibition *It's Pablo-matic* at the Brooklyn Museum in 2023—there is no genuine appetite for disruption in the present day. This discordance is abundantly apparent in Lauren Elkin's

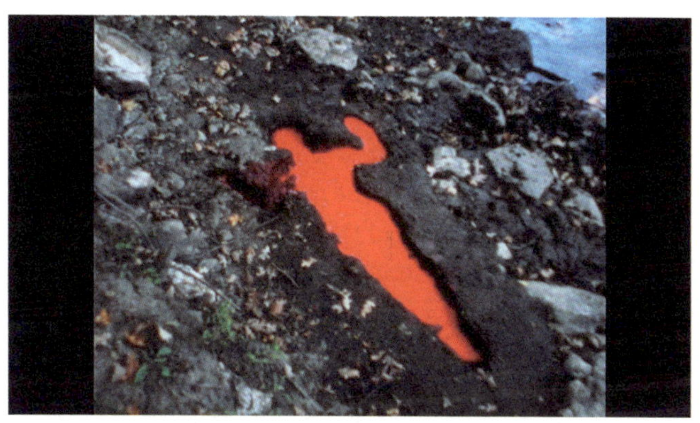

Still from Ana Mendieta, *Silueta Sangrienta* (1975)

2023 book *Art Monsters*. On the surface, the book proposes an embrace of queer and feminist artists who have broken the rules, stepped out of line, and acted monstrously in the pursuit of making art, ignoring the societal expectations that would place a limit on their creative and egoic aspirations. Yet Elkin takes no risks when naming her monsters. The roll call of artists and writers covered by the book—among them Julia Margaret Cameron, Virginia Woolf, Carolee Schneemann, Eva Hesse, Kathy Acker, and Paul B. Preciado—is familiar to universities, cultural magazines, museums, and galleries the world over, and is a more or less accepted list of what counts for politically aware good taste. Indeed, the most interesting aspect of Elkin's book is how careful the author is, in a book ostensibly about transgression, not to risk her own political credentials—and how ready she is to call out others who are deemed to have broken the rules.

Elkin goes out of her way to single out Dana Schutz, who provoked an almighty backlash when she presented *Open Casket* at the Whitney Biennale in 2017—a painting of the dead Emmett Till, a fourteen-year-old boy lynched by a racist mob in 1955. The display of the work kicked off one of the most notable moral battles of the last decade. That year, the theme of the Biennial was "racial tensions, economic inequities, and polarizing politics," and the way "these realities affect our senses of self and community." By the time it opened in March, Donald Trump had been sworn in as president for the first time, an executive order to build a wall on the Mexican border had been signed, Colin Kaepernick had been "taking the knee" for over six months, and half a million people in pink pussy hats had marched through the streets of Washington, DC.

The curators' intentions to confront viewers with the violence of systemic inequality took an unexpected turn when the show was buried under an avalanche of protests and press coverage relating to the inclusion of *Open Casket*. Schutz based the painting on a photograph of Till in an open coffin taken at his public funeral in Chicago. She treated the canvas like the glass window of the coffin, painting Till from the waist up in a black suit and white shirt, a red rose pinned to the waistband of his trousers. His head is surrounded by a yellow fabric that suggests a halo, his face rendered in a naive and partially abstract style that creates an insinuation of brutality but shies away from outright depiction, the tasteful brown, green, and red brushstrokes not so much evoking mutilated flesh or psychological turmoil as placing a fig leaf over the violence. It was not the only painting at the Biennale to depict the corpse of a Black person. Henry Taylor based *THE TIMES THAY AINT A CHANGING, FAST ENOUGH!* (2017) on video footage that Philando Castile's girlfriend had live-streamed in the aftermath of his shooting by a policeman in Minnesota in 2016. Taylor's painting avoided the opprobrium that Schutz faced, for the obvious reason, according to the logic of identity politics, that he is a Black man and not a white woman, thus making the subject of Castile's death rightfully his to paint. Yet like *Open Casket*, *THE TIMES* is an uncomfortably decorous depiction of murder. Painted in sunny greens, yellows, browns, and blues, its easy, pleasing aesthetic would not be amiss on the walls of a coworking space, beside the potted plants and coffee machine, if it weren't for the subject matter at hand.

The protests began with an artist named Parker Bright, who stood before *Open Casket* blocking the view, wearing a T-shirt with the words "Black Death Spectacle" written across the back. Things reached a fever pitch when an open letter to the Whitney's curators, written by the British artist Hannah Black, and cosigned by others, began circulating. "I am writing to ask you to remove Dana Schutz's painting 'Open Casket' and with the urgent recommendation that the painting be destroyed and not entered into any market or museum," Black wrote. She had pressed the free speech button, and what came next unfolded with a certain inevitability: comparisons to fascism and Nazi book burning; a heated debate over what was the greater risk to culture, cultural appropriation or calling for the destruction of art. A letter of apology purportedly written by Schutz also began circulating, listing the things she had done wrong, before it was revealed that her email account had been hacked and the letter was in fact a hoax.

In certain respects, Schutz's painting was a bland provocateur. Whatever we might think of it, she had not intended to cause offense. "My engagement with this image was through empathy with his mother," she would later say, along with a vapid statement about the pain of Till's mother being America's pain. Picking through the drama that unfolded in the wake of *Open Casket's* display, the writer Zadie Smith noted the painting's curious lack of power or presence, its strange nothingness. "I turned from the painting, not offended, not especially shocked or moved, not even terribly engaged by it, and walked with the children to the next room." Its lack of power likely contributed to its notoriety. Formally and psychologically timid, its tastefulness was grating, and it offered little resistance to the political narratives swirling in the ether, looking for somewhere to land: the unconscious bias and entitlement of white women (2017 was also the year in which the Karen meme originated on Reddit); a vampiric art world, feeding off the blood of the oppressed; the sickening hypocrisies of the do-gooder mentality; an America, and a Western world, poisoned to perversity by centuries of racism that it continuously fails to adequately confront; the white fetish for Black pain.

The debacle over *Open Casket* proved to be a turning point in the art world. Schutz's painting was not removed or destroyed, but the needle had shifted. Intended solidarities—however clunky—across identity groups would no longer be acceptable, unless the artist engaged in acts of public self-abnegation, performative gestures such as the giving-up of platforms, or in the policing of other people's behaviors. Subjects became the property of those groups who could claim relation.

Like a good student, Elkin had heeded these lessons. "I turn to Schutz's work," she writes, "to trace out a potential boundary, to ask whether there are places even the art monster cannot, in good faith, go. It is not enough simply to make work that offends people, claim it as transgressive, and step away from the easel." To be a feminist art monster, Elkin writes, "requires a bit more labor than that, a work of thought and perception, of looking and reflection and calling into question, work that I do not believe Schutz has done."

Never mind that Schutz had not meant for *Open Casket* to be "transgressive," or to cause offense. Never mind that it was painted broadly in the same spirit as Elkin's book was written, as a stylized attempt to publicly perform solidarity with marginalized groups to which the author may not belong. Fatally, for Schutz, she had made the painting without the required dose of self-consciousness and thus had broken the rules of Liberal Realism. In Elkin's words, she had not done the work to qualify as the right kind of art monster.

IV
Morality Is a Fickle Mistress

Liberal Realism may be facile and tiresome. It may be patronizing, paranoid, and self-serving. It may work against the possibility that art can become more than the sum of its parts. All of this, of course, is a terrible shame. But perhaps the greatest danger is that the rules about what counts as the moral high ground are liable to change. You may well think that taking a hit on the quality of cultural production is worthwhile if it helps to build a kinder and more welcoming society. But what happens when you don't agree with the moral code that happens to be in the ascendancy? What happens if that code discriminates against you, or the causes or people that you care for?

The logic that drives Liberal Realism is the same as that which underpins contemporary identity politics more broadly, whether its proponents are advocating for social-justice movements or clamoring for right-wing populism. Across the board, identity is increasingly treated as a mini nation-state, a thing with borders that must be patrolled and defended, founding myths that must be repeated, enemies who must be vanquished and heroes who must be worshipped. The culture produced by such a mindset is inevitably highly partisan, self-righteous, and morally censorious. The danger to the Left—or what remains of it in mainstream politics—is that the tools it cultivates for its own ends are often more successfully wielded by right-wing forces, as we have seen with the extraordinary resurgence of nationalist and patriarchal identities. It is one thing to argue that the master's tools can never successfully be wielded to dismantle the master's house. It is quite another to advertise a shiny collection of instruments designed to incite moral superiority and certitude and leave them on his doorstep.

Liberal Realism is the cultural arm of what is known in France as the "extreme center"—a type of politics exemplified by the administrations of Joe Biden, Keir Starmer, and Emmanuel Macron, as well as the presidential campaign of Kamala Harris. This brand of politics is only ever the other side of the coin to the recent wave of nationalism, those bellicose iterations of populism, exemplified by the MAGA and Brexit movements, that draw energy from condemning and ridiculing liberals as out-of-touch elites infected by the "woke mind virus," just as liberals draw energy from condemning them in turn as bigots, fascists, and Hitler-incarnates. It's a cynical dance in which both parties need and sustain each other, requiring as they do a perfect enemy to galvanize the faithful, a group of people to denigrate for their turpitude and corruption. Identifying such an enemy allows you to claim the moral high ground, to secure your own sense of self as on the "right side of history." Each side of the coin is bonded by, and dependent upon, its hatred of the other.

As David Graeber said in 2020, such a system compels us to choose from options presented as polar opposites, setting up "a situation where these are the only two viable political choices, because they both feed off and complement one another." Such a system demands that we look no further, imagine there is nothing more out there, no worldview that understands these poles as fundamentally symbiotic.

The difference, as Donald Trump's 2024 reelection as President of the United States shows us, is that the Right is able to instrumentalize this dynamic more successfully, in part because the lip service the extreme center pays to kindness and equality is by now demonstratively a lie, and because it has no other vision to sell. It has shown itself time and again to be a war-enabling political project that does little to better the lives of the majority, either at home or abroad, and is primarily interested in maintaining the political and economic consensus rather than making lives more livable. Indeed, its major selling point today is not being as bad as the alternative, an argument that is hardly inspiring, and which relies on the patronizing notion that those who vote against their own interests are motivated by bigoted sentiments and low intelligence.

If we limit the scope of the arts to propaganda and chastise any instance of cultural production when it goes off message, we must remain open to the possibility that the arts may become a vehicle for spreading right-wing messaging, too, along the very same lines. The hand-wringing at the appointment of the right-wing journalist Pietrangelo Buttafuoco as the director of the Venice Biennale by Giorgia Meloni, and the Right's recent efforts to gain ideological control over US universities, are indicators that a battle for culture—long considered a stronghold of liberalism—is well underway.

Despite its frequent claims to radicality and transgression, Liberal Realism is almost exclusively dependent on conservative cultural institutions, academia, and funding bodies for opportunity and affirmation. In part, this is because of the scale of professionalization in the arts over the past few decades—artists increasingly consider art-making a career, like any other, and follow the trail of money and opportunity—and partly due to the economy in which we live. To create any kind of genuinely alternative cultural movement, cheap living costs are required so that artists can build communities fueled by the desire for artistic progress rather than a need to climb the greasy pole of capital.

The problem with placing art in the hands of administrators and bureaucrats is that they will follow whatever is politically expedient. One day, taking sides in an armed conflict is encouraged, as evidenced by the many Ukrainian flags hoisted above Western art institutions after the Russian invasion. On another day such a display of solidarity is unthinkable, as we have seen in the absence of Palestinian flags raised in the wake of Israel's brutal war on Gaza, following the Hamas-led armed incursion of October 7, 2023. In this regard, the arts merely reflect the expediency that is the hallmark of the extreme center. When the importance of expediency emerges, Liberal Realism's concept of morality adapts accordingly, moving with the political and economic consensus and working to protect its own interests. The language of social justice and solidarity is all that remains, hollowed out of its previous meaning, available to use as a costume that can dress up any issue.

In the summer of 2022, I saw for myself how easily narratives of social justice and claims of victimhood can be flipped. I had traveled to Kassel for the opening of Documenta, that curator's Valhalla, that 45-million-euro extravaganza that comes around once every five years, like a comet that can only be seen from a sleepy city nestled deep in the German interior. Kassel is home to schnitzel chains and eighteenth-century architecture that has the look of expensive but not particularly delicious cakes. Since 1955, the city has also been home to an art quinquennial founded as part of the great postwar atonement for Germany's shame, a grand display intended to advertise the country's modern and international aspirations, its heartfelt wish to wrap its arms around its brother and sister nations, to wash the blood from its hands with the world as its witness, to show how changed it was from the country that organized the *Entartete Kunst* (Degenerate Art) exhibition and the book burnings, some of which took place in Kassel's central square.

This unlikely destination periodically becomes the center of the art world, hosting exhibitions organized by some of the most celebrated names in curation. But this iteration, Documenta 15, was advertised as very different from those that had come before it. For starters, it would reflect the spirit of the age: a time when both the individual and the concept of genius have been locked in the stocks for crimes of patriarchy, capitalism, and Western civilization, and everyone, from activists to the curators of conservative art institutions, hurls whatever they can in their direction; a time when public funding is geared toward supporting projects that promise benefits to local communities and tout their collaborative credentials; a time when the words "accessibility" and "inclusivity" reign, and no institution has a chance of receiving public funding without running outreach programs.

In the spirit of such an age, this Documenta aimed to be an entirely collective endeavor, a place for communities and workshops, where the art object (filthy fetish of consumerism) would finally be knocked off its plinth. There would be no curator (emblem of individualism), and the reigns would instead be handed over to the Jakarta-based artist collective Ruangrupa, who in turn invited other collectives, who in turn invited yet more collectives, and so on and so forth, until the total number of participants reached 1,500. Funds would be redistributed among these hundreds of collectives, and the focus would be on the marginalized and the Global South, a model of internationalism that was not intended to serve a Western audience but to sustain the participants' needs. This Documenta would be organized without a top-down model. A few years prior, such an approach would probably have been described as *rhizomatic*, but as the European canon had been shut away in the attic, like an embarrassing grandparent who can't be trusted not to say something appalling in front of guests, this year the phrase was *lumbung*, the Indonesian word for a collective rice barn, and a metaphor for how resources would be shared among communities of artists. "Make friends not art!" Ruangrupa proclaimed in the exhibition guidebook. At this Documenta, "art" would have second-class status, and the city's venues would instead be transformed into community hubs.

I walked through a room lined with corrugated metal to look like a shantytown, past a re-creation of a village hut, through a room full of photographic portraits of queer indigenous people from Aotearoa—installations in keeping with a pattern of funding artists who perform their ethnic or gender identities for a global network of institutions, a pattern that has been uncritically embraced in the past decade in the name of positive representation, and which risks turning the festival circuit into a kind of identity-political reboot of the *National Geographic*.

At the end of a day spent wandering around Documenta 15's sprawling venues, I arrived with some friends at a courtyard, where visitors had gathered for the opening night event—an S&M fetish party, run by the Mumbai-based collective Office Party HQ. A queue had formed, and excitement whistled through the crowd as news began to spread of people being turned away. Members of the collective were standing guard by the entrance, performing a kind of mash-up of club bouncer and border control—attempting to ascertain where people were from, and what their gender and sexuality were, and turning away anyone they didn't like the look of. Never mind the assumption that everyone looks exactly how they feel, and that people may not want to confide private information to hostile strangers high on the spectacle of authority. Never mind the unpleasantness of demanding that visitors effectively show their passports and gay cards in the name of creating a safe space.

Eventually my friends and I got past the checkpoint. We walked past a giant "code of conduct" printed on a slab of wood like the Ten Commandments, warning visitors not to talk to the DJ on pain of expulsion, and that they could be thrown out at any moment without explanation. Inside, the guests circulated awkwardly, wandering through plastic curtains and giggling nervously at the assortment of cheap whips and feathers that had been laid out, as if we were attending a hen party sponsored by Ann Summers. Taking in this LARP of a sex club, I was hit by a revelation. The fetish being catered to here had nothing to do with sex, but fed a different kind of power play entirely: the power to punish people, a kind of dominance justified by a spurious claim to moral superiority, a weaponized model of self-proclaimed victimhood with which to create and enforce rules. The following day, I returned to see a video Office Party HQ was screening in a nearby basement. It showed members of the collective rolling around in the dirt dressed in corsets and panties, offering their wrists up to be handcuffed by imaginary people—a strange, sexual fever dream of oppression performed by the previous night's police.

What happened next at Documenta 15 dominated the headlines for years to come. Days after it opened, a depiction of a Mossad agent with a pig's snout, and an Orthodox Jewish man with fangs wearing a bowler hat emblazoned with the letters SS, were spotted in a large mural created in 2002 by the Indonesian collective Taring Padi, on display in the public square outside the Fridericianum. The mural had been made in commemoration of the victims of General Suharto—the dictator responsible for the deaths of at least half a million people accused of harboring communist sympathies. Suharto's dictatorship was supported by Western forces fighting the Cold War, and by Israel. Mossad kept a station in Jakarta under the cover of a commercial company and provided military equipment to his regime.

Following the backlash against the mural, Taring Padi issued a response, apologizing for any offense caused, and offering an unconvincing defense—given the specificity of the symbolism—that animal caricatures were used throughout the mural and were not intended to be anti-Semitic. The mural was covered up, but it did little to quell the criticism. Nor did its eventual removal.

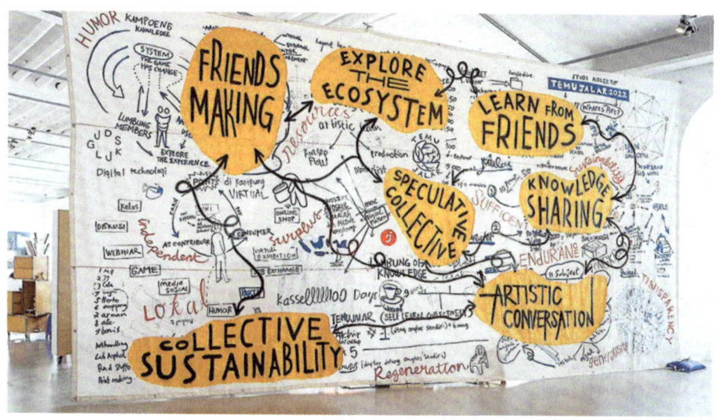

Gudskul banner, Fridericianum, Kassel, June 11, 2022. Photo: Nicolas Wefers

German politicians expressed their outrage, the Israeli embassy tweeted that "Documenta promotes Goebbels-style propaganda," and representatives of the Anne Frank Foundation visited to inspect the work on show and deemed the exhibition anti-Semitic. Artists including Hito Steyerl began retracting their work, the director of Documenta stood down, and the entire project fell to pieces as the world watched on.

Whether or not the inclusion of the mural was an oversight on behalf of the curators and the Documenta team, or whether the symbolism was something they had actively intended to present to audiences, remains unclear. But it was certainly incendiary—the equivalent of throwing a lit match into the forecourt of a gas station and not expecting it to go up in flames. In contrast, vandalism reported in relation to work by the Palestinian collective The Question of Funding did not provoke the same levels of international or domestic outrage from senior politicians or mainstream journalists, nor did the appearance of stickers bearing the words "Freedom not Islam! No compromise with barbarism! Fight Islam consistently!" There was certainly no room in the fallout for a discussion of global politics, of how the oppressed can, and frequently do, also act as oppressors, of the aftereffects of Israel's history of warmongering. Indeed, months before Documenta 15 opened, the inclusion of The Question of Funding had already set alarm bells ringing, as the very idea of Palestinian artists participating was equated with anti-Israeli and thus anti-Semitic politics—a view aired by everyone from splinter groups to prominent German newspapers. This asymmetry proved a grim foreshadowing of the political dynamic that would emerge in the wake of October 7, and the deplatforming and defunding of Palestinian artists, authors, and their supporters from events, awards, and jobs, as well as the refusal of visas, often for little more than the fact of their nationality, or their stated objection to the killing of Palestinian civilians.

V
What Is Lost

When applied to art, morality is a fickle thing. Those clamoring for exclusions and punishments in the name of the "good" may suddenly find themselves silenced or criminalized. This happened to Ruangrupa's Documenta 15. The enforcement of a ruthless moral code, and the expulsion of anyone who fell foul of it, was enacted with a similar zeal by those on either side of the divide. However, when state and media performed it, rather than a power-hungry artist collective organizing a phony sex club, the results were far more profound. This, surely, is not what we want from art: for it to be reduced to a tool for providing Public Service Announcements for whichever ideology is in the ascendancy, a means of humiliating or destroying political opposition.

What do we lose when art is swallowed by moral battles? When it becomes a way to advertise the good politics of individuals, galleries, and institutions, a means of cleaning up the past so that it suits the narratives of the present, an aid for telling whichever story happens to be palatable and expedient? For starters, we lose the capacity to think outside of present ideologies and to imagine other ways of being. These are the very kinds of cognitive skills we will need if we are to imagine futures beyond the crushing inevitability described by Mark Fisher, and the dogmatic and anti-intellectual model of art advanced by Liberal Realism, which encourages us to indulge in simplistic myths of heroes and villains, and to celebrate the triumph of flatness over depth, self-consciousness over curiosity, the known over the unknown. Because what is the value and purpose of art, after all, if not to transport us beyond our everyday realities, beyond the world as we think we know it, in order to open up the broad and mysterious spectrum of human experiences and drives, to enhance, rather than limit, our perception of the world around us?

The benefit of embracing moral ambivalence, of being against morality dominating art, is not merely the opportunity to indulge in the thrill of transgression, however valuable an experience that can be. It is to learn how to face that which we don't already know. It is to be able to look at an artwork, or watch a film, or read a book, and find value in questions raised rather than answers fed to us on a spoon. It is to encounter ambivalent emotions and sensations, to engage with art's capacity to enhance an understanding of our darkest impulses as well as our potential for goodness. This is what is so powerful about Chaïm Soutine's portraits of cooks and bellboys. The violence and tenderness they conjure, the combination of sweetness and perversity contained within a single image—sometimes, within a single brush mark—pushes the viewer to go beyond what they think they *ought* to feel, what they think they already know, and to experience a fundamental irresolution that contains within it something of the beauty and horror of being alive. If we fail to move beyond simplistic moral narratives, if we are content for art to exist as little more than a set of identity markers and political affiliations used to advertise ourselves to the world, art will lose its transcendent and transformative dimensions. As a consequence, we will destroy a path to better understanding ourselves and the world around us.

Acknowledgments

Thanks to Kristian Vistrup Madsen, for the conversations over the years; Izabella Scott, a trusted reader; *ArtReview*, *e-flux*, and other publications who published reviews and and essays that fed into this one; and Aaron, Jude, and the team at Floating Opera Press for helping to bring this essay to life.

Section I, Liberal Realism, was partially adapted with edits from "Queer: Some Notes on Art and Identity," published by *e-flux*, April 9, 2020; section III, Heroes and Villains, was partially adapted with edits from "Ana Mendieta Deserves Better Than a True-Crime Podcast," published by *ArtReview*, November 22, 2022.

Biography

Rosanna McLaughlin is a writer and editor who lives in East Sussex. She is the author of two books: *Double-Tracking* (Carcanet, 2019), a collection of satirical essays and short fiction, and the novel *Sinkhole* (Montez Press, 2023). She was formerly coeditor of *The White Review*.

Image Credits

P. 6
Chaïm Soutine, *Le Groom* (1925);
courtesy of bpk/CNAC-MNAM/
Philippe Migeat

P. 14
Hieronymus Bosch, *The Garden
of Earthly Delights* (1490–1500),
detail; courtesy of Wikimedia
Commons

P. 19
Still from *Tár* (2022); courtesy
of Universal Studios Licensing
LLC. © MMXXII Focus Features
LLC. All Rights Reserved

P. 25
Boris Eremeevich Vladimirski,
Roses for Stalin (1949)

P. 26
Andy Warhol, *A Woman's
Suicide* (1962); courtesy of bpk/
Kunstsammlung Nordrhein-
Westfalen, Düsseldorf

P. 35
Agesander, Athenodoros, and
Polydorus, *Laocoön and His
Sons* (ca. 27 BC–68 AD); courtesy
of Wikimedia Commons

P. 38
Artemisia Gentileschi, *Judith
Slaying Holofernes* (1611–12);
courtesy of Wikimedia Commons

P. 45
Ana Mendieta, *Silueta
Sangrienta* (1975), super 8 mm
film transferred to HD digital
video (color, silent); courtesy of
Galerie Lelong & Co., New
York, licensed by Artists Rights
Society (ARS), New York.
© The Estate of Ana Mendieta
Collection, LLC

P. 61
Gudskul banner, Fridericianum,
Kassel, June 11, 2022; courtesy of
the photographer. Photo: Nicolas
Wefers

Colophon

Series editor:
Aaron Bogart

Copyediting:
Louisa Elderton

Editorial assistance:
Jude Macannuco

Proofreading:
Nadia Egan

Graphic design:
Daniela Burger

Typesetting:
Vreni Knödler

Typeface:
Kelvin Avec Clair

Printing:
druckhaus köthen

Paper:
F-color Karton Feinkorn,
Munken Print White

Published by
Floating Opera Press
Hasenheide 9
10967 Berlin
www.floatingoperapress.com

ISBN 978-3-9826683-2-1

Printed in Germany